THE TUNNEL BORING MACHINE

Builds a Tunnel!

On the way into Miss Moxie's class, Cloe the TBM was always last.

The other kids would stare and be mean because Cloe was a tunnel boring machine.

"You're boring," they said. "You're big and you're slow."
"You aren't like us. You're dull. You should go."

"Come now," said Miss Moxie. "Pull up to your spots. There's work to be done and lessons to be taught."

"Class, it is my job to make dirty water clean. But there is a problem with my cleaning machine."

Even if the students dug deep really well,
the dirt around them always toppled and fell.

"I know I can do it!" yelled the shovel named Stu.
But it took far too long for his blade to get through.

"Well," Cloe said, from the back of the room, "could we build a big tunnel to get it to you?"

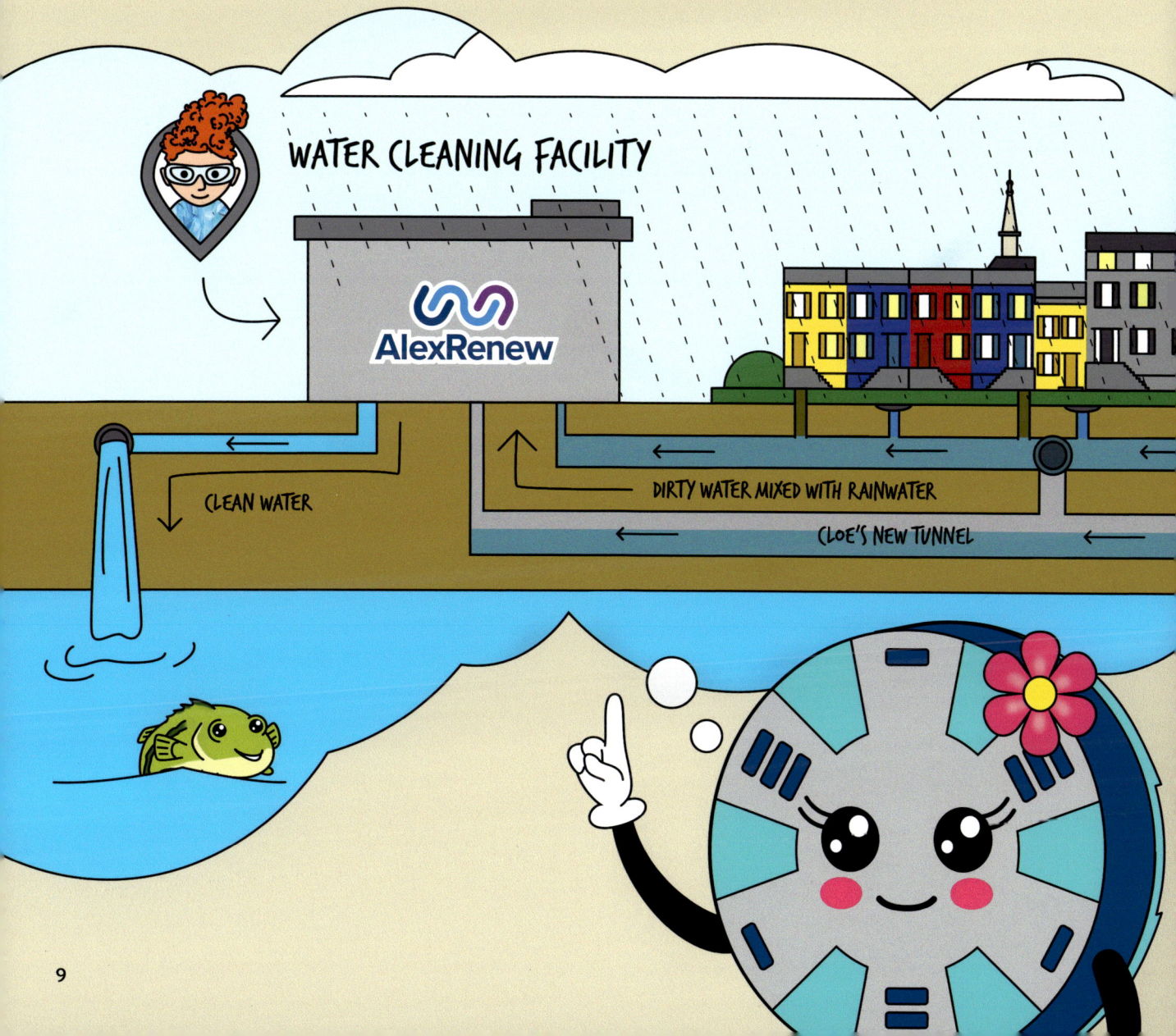

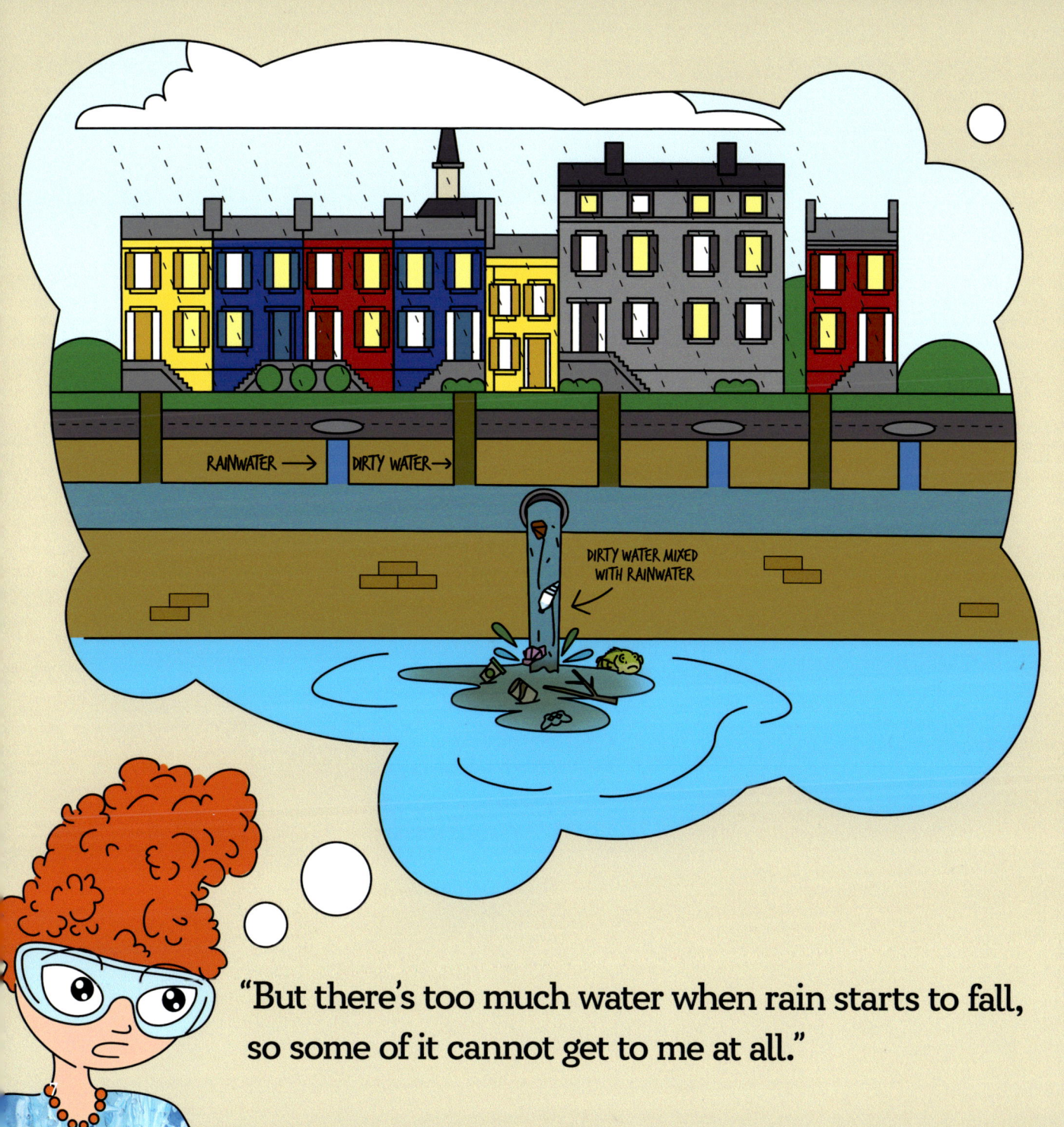

"I bring in dirty water used all over the city.
And, with my special mixture, it turns clean and pretty!"

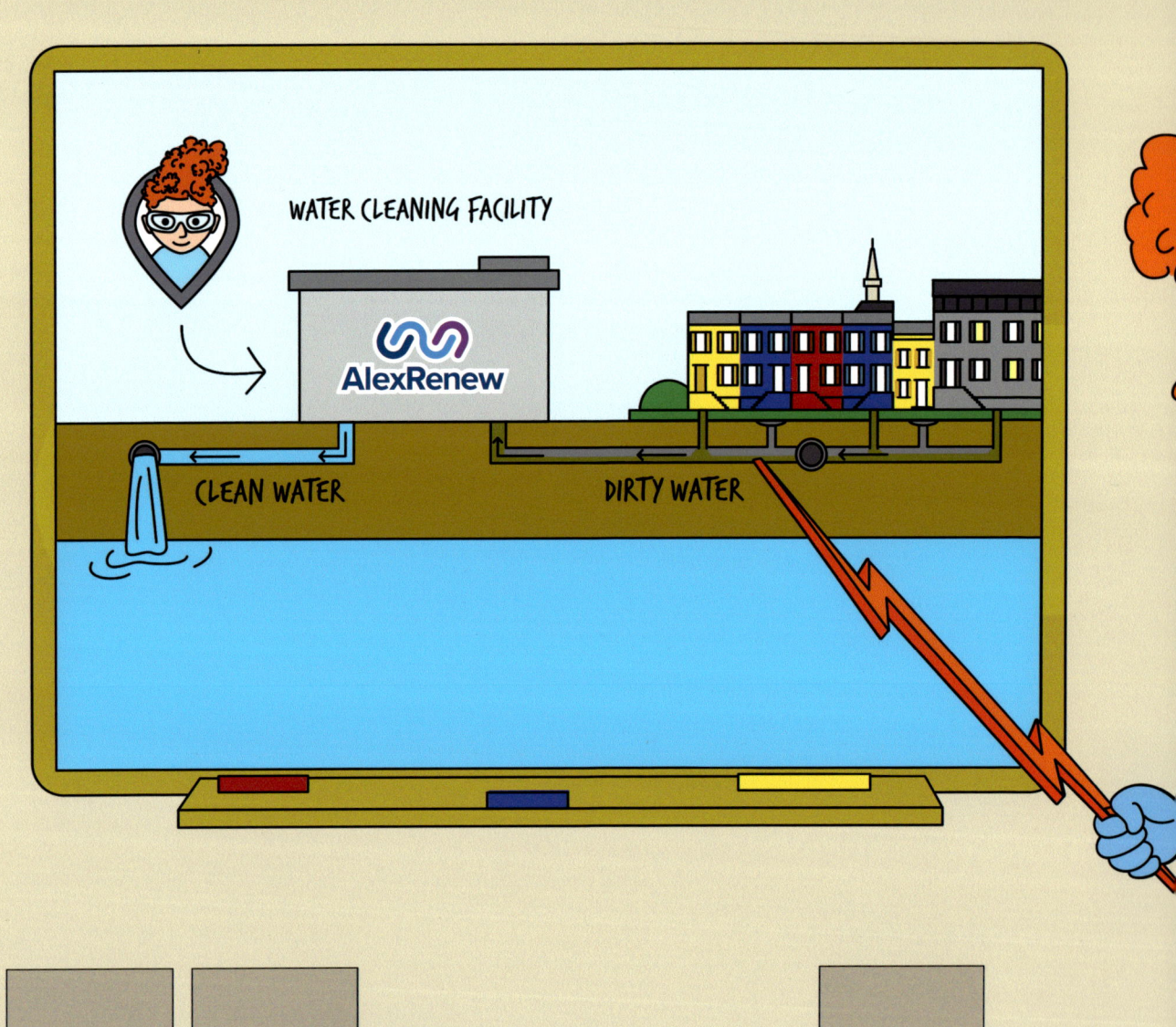

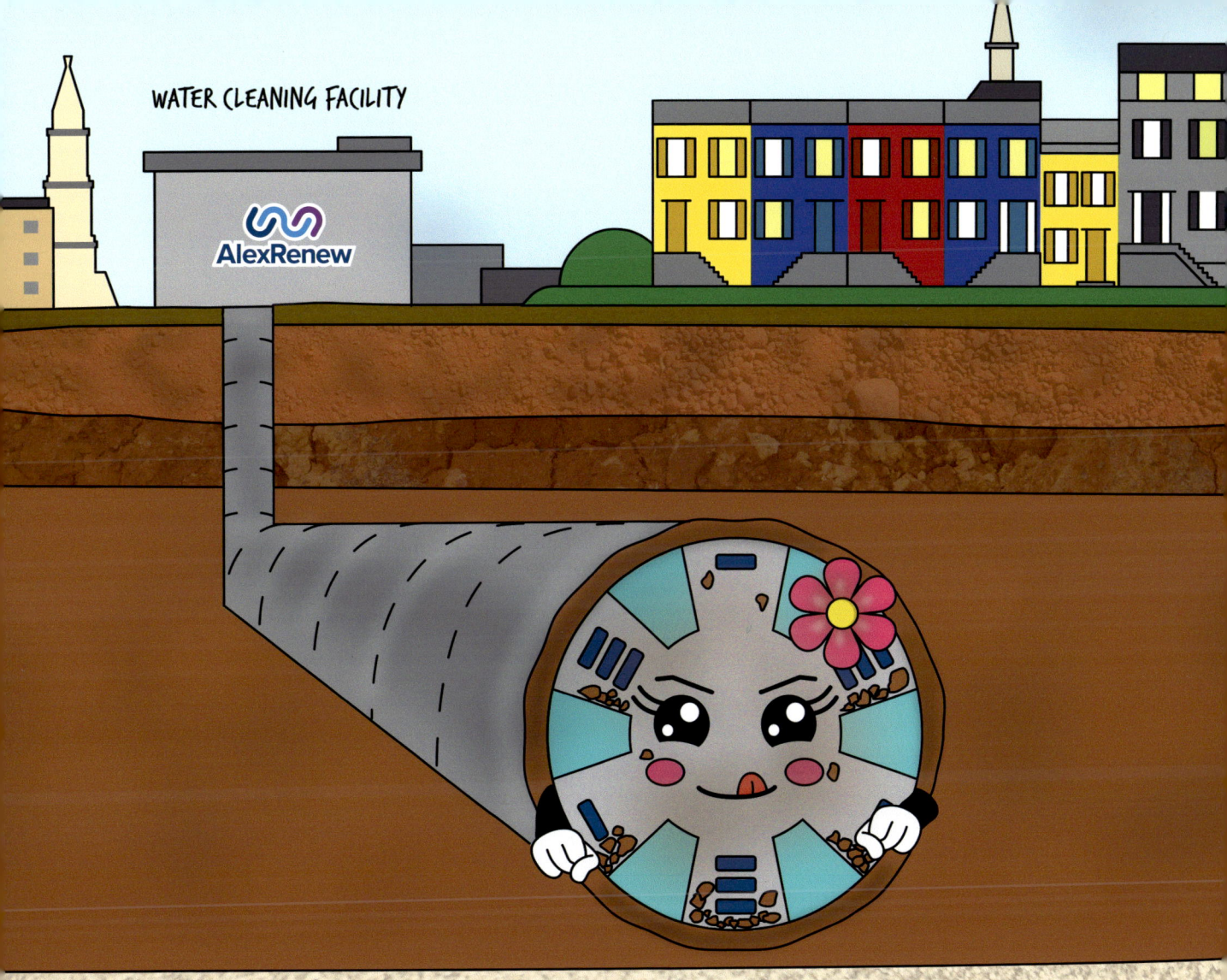

But look! While the others got tired and sad,
Cloe was digging like no one else had.

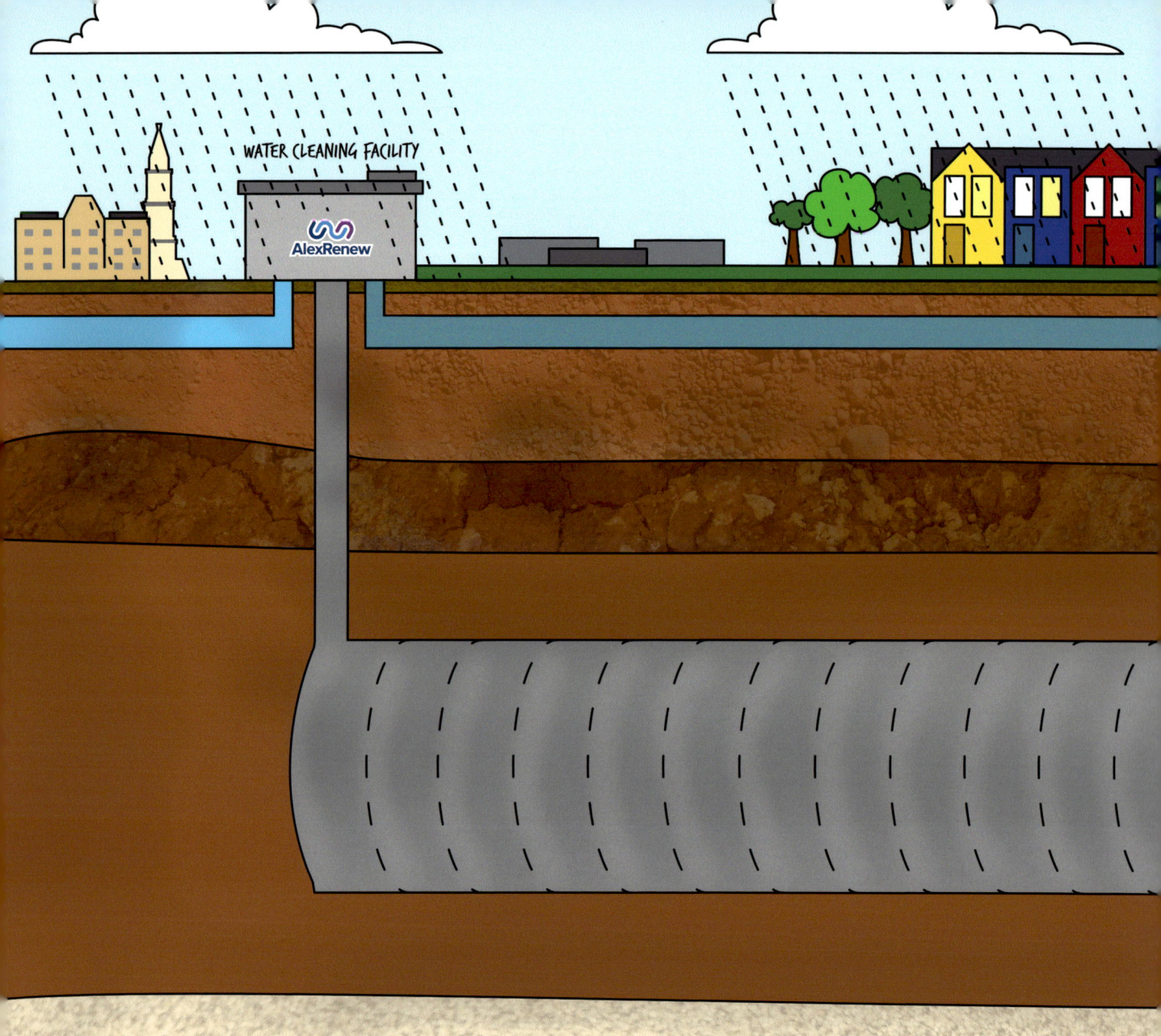

"My tunnel is strong," Cloe said, feeling proud.
"I know how to make them because I live underground."

"That's a great idea," said the Backhoe Brothers. "We'll scoop out a tunnel before all the others."

But, try as they might, the brothers could not.
They dug down a bit before their claws got caught.

And the fish could swim happily wherever they roamed.
Cloe took dirty water away from their home!

Moxie's Reading Recap

Words to Know

- **Clean Water:** Water that has been cleaned at AlexRenew's Water Cleaning Facility to be returned to the Potomac River
- **Dirty Water:** The Water that you (and everyone in Alexandria) flushes down the toilet, drips down the shower, or swirls down the sink
- **Rainwater:** The Water that falls from the sky during a rain, hail, or snow storm
- **TBM:** Short for "Tunnel Boring Machine," a big piece of equipment used to dig tunnels underground
- **Water Cleaning Facility:** AlexRenew's wastewater treatment plant, which uses processes, equipment, and people to clean dirty water every day from all over the city

Wildlife Common to Our Watershed

- **Barn Swallow:** A small species of bird that nests and feeds near water bodies like the Potomac River
- **Diamondback Terrapin:** A species of turtle that lives in rivers and streams on the East Coast, like the Potomac River and Hunting Creek
- **Largemouth Bass:** A species of fish that lives in the Potomac River and other waterways across Virginia

What's Under Your Feet in Alexandria?

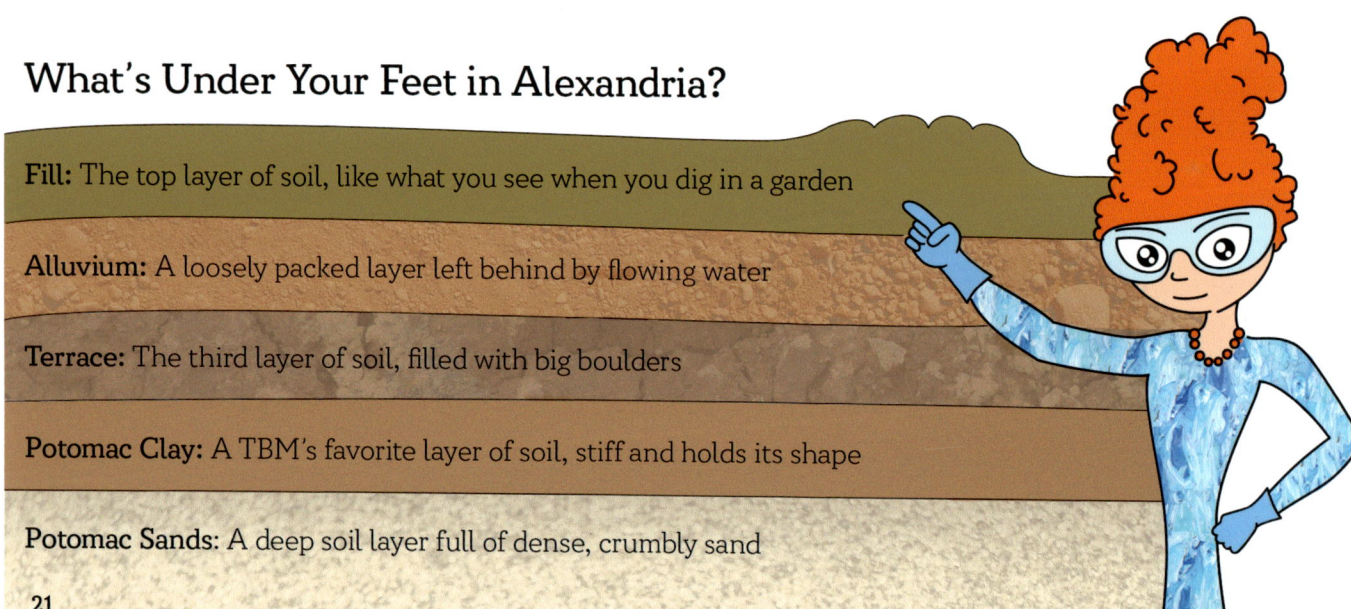

Fill: The top layer of soil, like what you see when you dig in a garden

Alluvium: A loosely packed layer left behind by flowing water

Terrace: The third layer of soil, filled with big boulders

Potomac Clay: A TBM's favorite layer of soil, stiff and holds its shape

Potomac Sands: A deep soil layer full of dense, crumbly sand